New Parents' Book of Quotes

Edited by Carol Kelly-Gangi

BARNES
& NOBLE
BOOKS
NEW YORK

A special thanks to my sister,
Barbara Kelly-Vergona, for her assistance,
helpful suggestions, and support.

The quotes in this book have been drawn from many
sources, and are assumed to be accurate as quoted in their
previously published forms. Although every effort has been
made to verify the quotes and sources, the publisher
cannot guarantee their perfect accuracy.

2003 Barnes & Noble Books

ISBN 0-7607-4071-2

Printed and bound in the United States of America

M 9 8 7 6 5 4 3 2

For John August and John Christopher
with love.

THE ONE THING THAT NEW PARENTS QUICKLY
discover is that babies don't come with any
instructions. It's definitely a case of on-the-job
training like you've never been through before.
All at once, you're confronted with everything
there is to do for this new little bundle—who has
managed to take over your heart and your home
at the same time.

New Parent's Book of Quotes offers first-time
parents more than two hundred quotations in
categories that speak to many of the stages
parents encounter in their new and wonderful
role. There are selections from writers and
humorists, pediatricians and midwives, educators
and entertainers, politicians and philosophers,
and even from youngsters themselves. But whatever their other occupations, the great majority of
contributors are here first and foremost because
they are parents—who can offer reassuring words
of experience on everything from baby-proofing

to surviving the teenage years. Anna Quindlen and Madeleine L'Engle recall the first miraculous moments with their newborns; Bill Cosby and David Steinberg offer insights into the universal anxieties that new parents face; Ralph Waldo Emerson and Deepak Chopra marvel at the wonder of children; and Erma Bombeck and Barbara Bush ponder the meaning of family.

So take a deep breath. It's our hope that *New Parent's Book of Quotes* will brace you, encourage you, and in some small way help to prepare you for one of life's great journeys. And when all else fails, remember the words of Dr. Benjamin Spock, "Trust yourself. You know more than you think you do."

—CAROL KELLY-GANGI
Rumson, New Jersey, 2003

Are We Ready for This?

Making the decision to have a child—it's momentous. It is to decide forever to have your heart go walking outside your body.

—ELIZABETH STONE, writer

A baby is God's opinion that the world should go on.

—CARL SANDBURG, writer

Having a child is surely the most beautifully irrational act that two people in love can commit.

—BILL COSBY, entertainer and writer

Most of us become parents long before we have stopped being children.

—MIGNON MCLAUGHLIN, journalist

If men had to have babies they would only ever have one each.

—DIANA, PRINCESS OF WALES

If you really love your wife, her pregnancy is a time to test your attention span. You have to pay attention when she says, "It's moving! Wake up and feel it!" You have to respond as if she's pointing out a replay of a touchdown pass.

—BILL COSBY, entertainer and writer

The old system of having a baby was much better than the new system, the old system being characterized by the fact that the man didn't have to watch.

—DAVE BARRY, writer and humorist

Although the lifestyle changes may be greater or lesser, depending on how you and your spouse decide to order your priorities, it's true that your life is never going to be the same again once your "two" becomes "three." But as some parts of your world become more constricted, others will open up. You may find yourself reborn with your baby's birth. And this new life may turn out to be the best yet.

—ARLENE EISENBERG, HEIDI E. MURKOFF,
AND SANDEE E. HATHAWAY,
What To Expect When You're Expecting

Bringing a child into the world is the greatest act of hope there is.

—LOUISE HART, writer and poet

And Baby
Makes Three

Your baby's first cry is the one you hear in the delivery room, the triumphant, tension-shattering sound that says, "I'm here, I'm breathing, I'm alive!"

—KATHERINE KARLSRUD, physician and writer

My child looked at me and I looked back at him in the delivery room, and I realized that out of a sea of infinite possibilities it had come down to this: a specific person, born on the hottest day of the year, conceived on a Christmas Eve, made by his father and me miraculously from scratch.

—ANNA QUINDLEN, writer

I looked at this tiny, perfect creature and it was as though a light switch had been turned on. A great rush of love flooded out of me.

—MADELEINE L'ENGLE, writer and educator

I remember leaving the hospital...thinking, "Wait, are they going to let me just walk off with him? I don't know beans about babies! I don't have a license to do this. [We're] just amateurs."

—ANNE TYLER, novelist

She held my attention like a fiery constellation. Her eyes bewitched me. Her first smile caused me and Jon to waltz around the room with the baby between us. We were besotted with her, the first parents in history.

—ERICA JONG, *Fear of Fifty*

Tonight I see how scared I am. There is so much to do for this little creature who screams and wriggles.

—DAVID STEINBERG, comedian and writer

Parents experience intense and often polar and confusing emotions upon the birth of a baby. Exhilaration, relief, anxiety, love, anger, loneliness, joy, and doubt can all arise. The baby is a powerful elicitor of the range of parent's own emotional strengths and vulnerabilities.

—T. BERRY BRAZELTON AND STANLEY I. GREENSPAN, pediatricians and writers

When you are drawing up your list of life's miracles, you might place near the top of the list the first moment your baby smiles at you.

—BOB GREENE, novelist and columnist

One thing about having a baby, is that each step of the way you simply cannot imagine loving him more than you already do, because you are bursting with love, loving as much as you are humanly capable of—and then you do, you love him even more.

—ANNE LAMOTT, writer

When you have a baby, you set off an explosion in your marriage, and when the dust settles, your marriage is different from what it was. Not better, necessarily; not worse, necessarily; but different.

—NORA EPHRON, screenwriter

New parents quickly learn that raising children is kind of desperate improvisation.

—BILL COSBY, entertainer and writer

Before the baby came you may have strived to maintain tight and rational control of your life. With a baby, however, much of your time will be spent in spontaneous activities, requiring that you reach blindly into your bag of intuitions and come up with a suitable reaction on the spot.

—Daniel N. Stern and Nadia Bruschweiler,
physicians and writers

Baby's room...must have wallpaper with clowns holding blue, red, and green balloons. Baby's room should be close enough to your room so that you can hear baby cry, unless you want to get some sleep, in which case baby's room should be in Peru.

—Dave Barry, writer and humorist

Six weeks after Ben's birth my obstetrician declared me ready to resume sexual relations. Whatever that meant.

—Roberta Israeloff, writer and columnist

Everything about a new family takes time.

—Judy Blume, writer

People who say they sleep like a baby usually don't have one.

—Leo J. Burke, humorist

Our life was one long conversation about how tiring our days were.

—Roberta Israeloff, writer and columnist

Make a threesome.... As time alone with each other becomes a more and more precious and elusive commodity, concentrate on spending more time together as a family—stretching that mother-baby twosome into a cozy threesome—which you may find will strengthen the bonds between you as a couple. Pitching in with baby care will give your wife more time to devote to you, while giving you less inclination (and energy) to feel jealous.

—Arlene Eisenberg, Heidi E. Murkoff, and Sandee E. Hathaway, *What To Expect The First Year*

Mothers risk alienating their mates if they expect them to hold or care for the baby exactly as they do. Fathers who are constantly criticized or corrected may lose interest in handling the baby, and this is a loss for everyone. The cycle is a dangerous one. Now the same mother feels bitter because she is no longer getting any help at home.

—Cathy Rindner Tempelsman, journalist

Men will now get up and walk with the baby in the middle of the night, change its diapers, and give it a bottle, but in their heart of hearts they still think they shouldn't have to.

—RITA RUDNER, comedian and writer

One of the most important things to remember about infant care is: never change diapers in midstream.

—DON MARQUIS, humorist

Changing a diaper is a lot like getting a present from your grandmother—you're not sure what you've got but you're pretty sure you're not going to like it.

—JEFF FOXWORTHY, comedian

"There's nothing to worry about" is a typical example of the kind of easy-for-you-to-say remarks that pediatricians like to make.

—DAVE BARRY, writer and humorist

For the first six months or so, your opponent has been unable to escape. Alas, the rules are about to change drastically.... The enemy is now mobile.

—PETER MAYLE, writer

A man finds out what is meant by a spitting image when he tries to feed cereal to his infant.

—IMOGENE FEY, *Violets and Vinegar*

Having children is like having a bowling alley installed in your brain.

—MARTIN MULL, comedian

You can disarm the coffee table by clearing off the top and taping foam rubber padding 'round the sharp edges…this style is known as "Infant Provincial."

—PETER MAYLE, writer

The best time for parents to put the children to bed is while they still have the strength.

—ANONYMOUS

The one thing children wear out faster than shoes is parents.

—JOHN J. PLOMP, motivational writer

Whenever we take a trip, we have to enlist the help of thirteen sherpas, a chauffeur, two maids and a nanny—and that's only for the baby's luggage.

—GINGER HINCHMAN, geomorphologist

A baby enters your home and makes so much noise for twenty years you can hardly stand it—then departs, leaving the house so silent you think you'll go mad.

—Dr. J. A. Holmes

He's my wonderful, precious little Buddha. He eats like a champion. He sleeps peacefully—and he's the apple of his daddy's eye.

—Sharon Stone, actor

You don't want to leave home in the morning and you can't wait to get home at night. She's a year and a half and she's changing all the time.

—John Goodman, actor

Babies are more trouble than you thought, and more wonderful.

—CHARLES OSGOOD, journalist

The Wonder
of Kids

No one has yet fully realized the wealth of sympathy, kindness and generosity hidden in the soul of a child.

—EMMA GOLDMAN, anarchist and writer

We find a delight in the beauty and happiness of children that makes the heart too big for the body.

—RALPH WALDO EMERSON, writer and philosopher

The most sensitive, most delicate of instruments is the mind of a little child!

—HENRY HANDEL RICHARDSON, writer

dy lies on
mp, roll, and
me is relatively
es: The child may
e pounds and must
either is the child per-
s face or jump from an
sofa or coffee table.

—STAN AND JAN BERENSTAIN,
and creators of the Berenstain Bears

When a child plays, he is the manipulator; makes do with whatever is at hand. His imag tion transforms the commonplace into the less. A wooden clothespin, rescued from the kitchen table and wrapped in a dis becomes a baby; a penny thrust under a becomes a buried treasure.

—EDA LESHAN, writer a

Kids are your standing excuse to kinds of decidedly unadult behav down to make snow angels whe you or speaking in a Donald D

As we get older it seems we lose to express ourselves as purely. Little chil a way of reminding us of our original purpose: joy.

—MARIE OSMOND, entertainer

You don't really understand human nature unless you know why a child on a merry-go-round will wave at his parents every time around—and why his parents will always wave back.

—WILLIAM D. TAMMEUS, columnist and writ

Jump on Daddy. A game in which Dad the floor and suffers his child to ju climb on him at will. While this g unstructured, there are some ru not weigh more than thirty-fi remove his or her shoes. mitted to sit on Dadd elevated point like th

writers

Children are young, but they're not naîve. And they're honest. They're not going to keep awake if the story is boring. When they get excited you can see it in their eyes.

—CHINUA ACHEBE, novelist

What silent wonder is waked in the boy by blowing bubbles from soap and water with a pipe.

—RALPH WALDO EMERSON, writer and philosopher

Any adult who spends even fifteen minutes with a child outdoors finds himself drawn back to his own childhood, like Alice falling down the rabbit hole.

—SHARON MACLATCHIE, writer

Children's playthings are not sports and should be deemed as their most serious actions.

—MONTAIGNE, essayist

Play is often talked about as if it were a relief from serious learning. But for children play is serious learning. Play is really the work of childhood.

—FRED ROGERS, TV personality

Glued to the top of the box are twenty-three X's and O's made out of macaroni...the treasures of King Tut are nothing in the face of this.

—ROBERT FULGHUM, writer and artist

Having a young child explain something exciting he has seen is the finest example of communication you will ever hear or see.

—BOB TALBERT, writer

There are no seven wonders of the world in the eyes of a child. There are seven million.

—Walt Streightiff, writer

The monster under the bed finally arrived at our house the other night. I've been waiting for him to show up for four years.

—Anna Quindlen, writer

There is a garden in every childhood, an enchanted place where colors are brighter, the air softer, and the morning more fragrant than ever again.

—Elizabeth Lawrence, writer and columnist

Children display tremendous vitality and rush at every day with open arms.

—Dr. Deepak Chopra, physician and writer

Cherishing children is the mark of civilized society.

—JOAN GANZ COONEY, children's TV producer

From the
Mouths of Babes

Don't bite the hand that has your allowance in it.

—PAUL DICKSON, writer,
quoting a youngster named Lois

During this past Christmas while I was on a shopping spree in a department store I heard a little five-year-old talking to his mother on the down escalator. He said, "Mommy, what do they do when the basement gets full of steps?"

—HAL LINDEN, actor

"What do you think your daddy does best?"
  I asked one young man of five.
"Fall asleep in the chair," he replied.

—BILL COSBY, entertainer and writer

Even if I'm bad my dad has to still like me because I am in his family. I think it's a law.

—STUART HAMPLE, writer,
quoting a youngster named Alison

I've learned that just when I get my room the way I like it, Mom makes me clean it up.

—H. JACKSON BROWN, JR., writer,
quoting a thirteen-year-old youngster

My 3-year-old son frequently comments on his grandmother's wrinkles. Once, after taking a long bath, he noticed his fingers had shriveled up. I explained that he had stayed in the water too long. He said, "Grandma must put her face under the water for a long time when she takes a bath."

—NANETTE JOHANSEN, quoted in *Parents* magazine

There are no seven wonders of the world in the eyes of a child. There are seven million.

—WALT STREIGHTIFF, writer

The monster under the bed finally arrived at our house the other night. I've been waiting for him to show up for four years.

—ANNA QUINDLEN, writer

There is a garden in every childhood, an enchanted place where colors are brighter, the air softer, and the morning more fragrant than ever again.

—ELIZABETH LAWRENCE, writer and columnist

Children display tremendous vitality and rush at every day with open arms.

—DR. DEEPAK CHOPRA, physician and writer

Cherishing children is the mark of civilized society.

—Joan Ganz Cooney, children's TV producer

No one has yet fully realized the wealth of sympathy, kindness and generosity hidden in the soul of a child.

—EMMA GOLDMAN, anarchist and writer

We find a delight in the beauty and happiness of children that makes the heart too big for the body.

—RALPH WALDO EMERSON, writer and philosopher

The most sensitive, most delicate of instruments is the mind of a little child!

—HENRY HANDEL RICHARDSON, writer

When a child plays, he is the manipulator; he makes do with whatever is at hand. His imagination transforms the commonplace into the priceless. A wooden clothespin, rescued from under the kitchen table and wrapped in a dishcloth, becomes a baby; a penny thrust under a cushion becomes a buried treasure.

—EDA LeSHAN, writer and educator

Kids are your standing excuse to indulge in all kinds of decidedly unadult behavior, like flopping down to make snow angels when the spirit moves you or speaking in a Donald Duck voice.

—PEG ROSEN, writer

As we get older it seems we lose faith in our ability to express ourselves as purely. Little children have a way of reminding us of our original purpose: joy.

—MARIE OSMOND, entertainer

Just the other morning I caught myself looking at my children for the pure pleasure of it.

—PHYLLIS THEROUX, columnist and writer

One of the most delightful things about having children is experiencing the miracle of their development, watching the delight, innocence, and expression as they capture the newness in each experience, and sharing in the laughter of their play.

—ANNE K. BLOCKER, registered dietitian and writer

Every day you wake up to discover a slightly different person sleeping in that cradle, that crib, that bottom bunk, that dinosaur sleeping bag.

—JOYCE MAYNARD, writer and journalist

You don't really understand human nature unless you know why a child on a merry-go-round will wave at his parents every time around—and why his parents will always wave back.

—WILLIAM D. TAMMEUS, columnist and writer

Jump on Daddy. A game in which Daddy lies on the floor and suffers his child to jump, roll, and climb on him at will. While this game is relatively unstructured, there are some rules: The child may not weigh more than thirty-five pounds and must remove his or her shoes. Neither is the child permitted to sit on Daddy's face or jump from an elevated point like the sofa or coffee table.

—STAN AND JAN BERENSTAIN,
writers and creators of the Berenstain Bears

It's a family joke that when I was a tiny child I turned from the window out of which I was watching a snowstorm, and hopefully asked, "Momma, do we believe in winter?"

—PHILIP ROTH, novelist

I've learned that you can't hide a piece of broccoli in your glass of milk.

—H. JACKSON BROWN, JR., writer,
quoting a seven-year-old youngster

One recent morning, I overheard this poignant exchange between and father and his five-year-old son.

"I want my lunch," the boy proclaimed.

To which his father replied, "Well, how do you *ask* for it?"

"Like this: *I want my lunch.*"

—BILL COSBY, entertainer and writer

At a restaurant one night, the waitress was sweet-talking my 5-year-old son, Josh. "Can I take you home with me?" she teased. Josh considered her proposal, then replied, "No, but you can take my dad. He snores, and he sleeps naked."

—LAURA CHRISTIANSON, quoted in *Parents* magazine

Terrific Teens

Don't worry over your children! There are certain fool stages every child must pass through. Sit tight and wait!

—Dr. Frank Crane, writer

Parents should never have to share a telephone with their teenagers.

—Susan Hyde, writer

The cross that all children must bear is having parents who aren't even conscious of embarrassing them in the first place.

—Phyllis Theroux, columnist and writer

Let your child be the teenager he or she wants to be, not the adolescent you were or wish you had been.

—Laurence Steinberg and Ann Levine, writers

Remember that when in their teens children need more love, more companionship, more sympathy, and more attention than they ever needed before or will ever need again.

—Dr. Frank Crane, writer

Don't be afraid to be boss. Children are constantly testing, attempting to see how much they can get away with—how far you will let them go—and they secretly hope you will not let them go too far.... Accept the fact that there will be moments when your children will hate you. This is normal and natural. But how a child handles hate may determine whether he will go to Harvard or San Quentin.

—Ann Landers, advice columnist

Don't let yourself forget what it's like to be sixteen.

—Anonymous

A baby-sitter is a teenager who comes in to act like an adult while the adults go out and act like teenagers.

—ANONYMOUS

Never allow your child to call you by your first name. He hasn't known you long enough.

—FRAN LEBOWITZ, journalist

The conflict between the need to belong to a group and the need to be seen as unique and individual is the dominant struggle of adolescence.

—JEANNE ELIUM AND DON ELIUM, writers and talk-show hosts

Teenagers are people who express a burning desire to be different by dressing exactly alike.

—ANONYMOUS

I have found the best way to give advice to your children is to find out what they want and then advise them to do it.

—HARRY S TRUMAN,
33rd president of the United States

Adolescence begins when children stop asking questions—because they know all the answers.

—EVAN ESAR, humorist

Telling a teenager the facts of life is like giving a fish a bath.

—ARNOLD H. GLASOW, writer and humorist

If your teenager doesn't think you're a real embarrassment and a hard-nosed bore, you're probably not doing your job.

—ANONYMOUS

My mother had a great deal of trouble with me, but I think she enjoyed it.

—MARK TWAIN, writer and humorist

Oh, to be only half as wonderful as my child thought I was when he was small, and only half as stupid as my teenager now thinks I am.

—REBECCA RICHARDS, writer

The best way to keep children at home is to make the home atmosphere pleasant, and let the air out of the tires.

—DOROTHY PARKER, writer

You know your children are growing up when they stop asking where they came from and refuse to tell you where they're going.

—P. O'BRIEN, humorist

It is frequently said that children do not know the value of money. This is only partially true. They do not know the value of your money. Their money, they know the value of.

—JUDY MARKEY, writer and humorist

If you want to recapture your youth, just cut off his allowance.

—AL BERNSTEIN, humorist

Few things are more satisfying than seeing your children have teenagers of their own.

—DOUG LARSON, writer and humorist

Adolescence is perhaps nature's way of preparing parents to welcome the empty nest

—KAREN SAVAGE AND PATRICIA ADAMS
in *The Good Stepmother*

Don't laugh at a youth for his affectations; he is only trying on one face after another to find a face of his own.

—LOGAN PEARSALL SMITH, essayist

Family Matters

In one's family, respect and listening are the sources of harmony.

—BUDDHA

Family faces are magic mirrors. Looking at people who belong to us, we see the past, present and future.

—GAIL LUMET BUCKLEY, journalist and writer

The family. We were a strange little band of characters trudging through life sharing diseases and toothpaste, coveting one another's desserts, hiding shampoo, borrowing money, locking each other out of our rooms, inflicting pain and kissing to heal it in the same instant, loving, laughing, defending, and trying to figure out the common thread that bound us all together.

—ERMA BOMBECK, writer and humorist

Family: A unit composed not only of children, but of men, women, an occasional animal, and the common cold.

—OGDEN NASH, humorist

Having family responsibilities and concerns just has to make you a more understanding person.

—SANDRA DAY O'CONNOR, Supreme Court Justice

There's no such thing as fun for the whole family.

—JERRY SEINFELD, comedian

A family vacation is one where you arrive with five bags, four kids and seven I-thought-you-packed-its.

—IVERN BALL, humorist

To us, family means putting your arms around each other and being there.

—BARBARA BUSH, first lady

I think a dysfunctional family is any family with more than one person in it.

—MARY KARR, writer

He that has no fools, knaves nor beggars in his family was begot by a flash of lightning.

—THOMAS FULLER, physician and writer

No matter how much you disagree with your kin, if you are a thoroughbred you will not discuss their shortcomings with the neighbors.

—TOM THOMPSON, writer

One of the oldest human needs is having some-
one to wonder where you are when you don't
come home at night.

—Margaret Mead, anthropologist and writer

Blood's thicker than water, and when one's in
trouble, best to seek out a relative's open arms.

—Euripides, Greek playwright

Families with babies and families without babies
are sorry for each other.

—Edgar Watson Howe, journalist and writer

Having one child makes you a parent; having two
you are a referee.

—David Frost, journalist and writer

The first child is made of glass, the second porcelain, the rest of rubber, steel and granite.

—RICHARD J. NEEDHAM, politician and businessman

The beauty of "spacing" children many years apart lies in the fact that parents have time to learn the mistakes that were made with the older ones—which permits them to make exactly the opposite mistakes with the younger ones.

—SYDNEY J. HARRIS, journalist and writer

There comes a time in all children's lives when they notice that their families aren't perfect.

—PHYLLIS THEROUX, columnist and writer

The happiest moments of my life have been the few which I have passed at home in the bosom of my family.

—THOMAS JEFFERSON,
3rd president of the United States

Family jokes, though rightly cursed by strangers, are the bond that keeps most families alive.

—STELLA BENSON, novelist

Dinner together is one of the absolute critical symbols in the cohesion of the family.

—JOHN R. KELLY, journalist

Family life! The United Nations is child's play compared to the tugs and splits and need to understand and forgive in any family.

—MAY SARTON, poet and writer

Homes are built on the foundation of wisdom and understanding. Where there is knowledge, the rooms are furnished with valuable, learning things.

—PROVERBS

Home is the place where, when you have to go there, they have to take you in.

—ROBERT FROST, poet

Home is a place you grow up wanting to leave, and grow old wanting to get back to.

—JOHN ED PEARCE, journalist and writer

Very often we travel the world over in search of what we need and return home to find it.

—GEORGE MOORE, philosopher

Keeping house is like threading beads on a string with no knot at the end.

—Anonymous

I don't know what liberation can do about it, but even when the man helps, a woman's work is never done.

—Beryl Pfizer, journalist and writer

You become about as exciting as your food blender. The kids come in, look you right in the eye, and ask if anybody's home.

—Erma Bombeck, writer and humorist

The most remarkable thing about my mother is that for thirty years she served the family nothing but leftovers. The original meal has never been found.

—Calvin Trillan, journalist and writer

Fond as we are of our loved ones, there comes at times during their absence an unexplained peace.

—ANNE SHAW, writer

There are several ways in which to apportion the family income, all of them unsatisfactory.

—ROBERT BENCHLEY, humorist and actor

The family—that dear octopus from whose tentacles we never quite escape.

—DODIE SMITH, writer

Call it a clan, call it a network, call it a tribe, call it a family. Whatever you call it, whoever you are, you need one.

—JANE HOWARD, journalist and writer

On Parenthood...

No commitment in this whole world demands quite as much as bringing up children.

—JANENE WOLSEY BAADSGAARD, writer and counselor

Parenthood remains the greatest single preserve of the amateur.

—ALVIN TOFFLER, *Future Shock*

Parenthood is like a bowl of bing cherries—rich, sweet, and occasionally the pits. The reason that no one, heretofore, has revealed its dark secrets should be obvious. If our kids knew what raising kids was really like, we'd never have any grandchildren.

—STAN AND JAN BERENSTAIN,
writers and creators of the Berenstain Bears

Being a parent was, I had discovered, an endlessly demanding profession. At times I could hardly keep my chin up, so exhaustive were the demands. At other times the rewards were extraordinary— the sight, sound and smell of my children were miracle drugs that filled me with euphoria and significance.

—PHYLLIS THEROUX, columnist and writer

A husband and wife are a parenting team—each has an important and unique contribution to make to their child's development. They need to trust each other, respect each other's unique role, and help each other in times of stress. The most important thing you and your husband can do for your baby is to love one another.

—WILLIAM SEARS, pediatrician and writer

The true joy of parenting comes when we are empowered and can follow our own inner voice of guidance. Keep your eyes open, become informed; consider all options, all styles of parenting. Then make decisions about what's right for you and your family.

—TRACY HOGG, registered nurse, midwife, and writer

Parents owe their children a set of decent standards and solid moral values around which to build a life.

—ANN LANDERS, advice columnist

There are times when parenthood seems like nothing but feeding the mouth that bites you.

—PETER DE VRIES, novelist and humorist

Before I got married I had six theories about bringing up children; now I have six children and no theories.

—John Wilmot, British noble

The thing that impresses me most about Americans is the way parents obey their children.

—Edward VIII, Duke of Windsor

It is a mystery why adults expect perfection from children. Few grown-ups can get through a whole day without making a mistake.

—Marcelene Cox, columnist

We never know the love of our parents for us till we have become parents.

—Henry Ward Beecher, cleric

You learn that taking care of yourself is something you do in order to take care of the child. You have to keep yourself alive so that they can rely on you. You have to give them a consistent environment where they can be fed and bathed and clothed and entertained and educated and loved and not necessarily in that order.

—CARRIE FISHER, actor

Parenthood is quite a long word. I expect it contains the rest of my life.

—KAREN SCOTT BOATES, writer

Parenthood: the state of being better chaperoned than you were pre-marriage.

—ANONYMOUS

The most important thing a father can do for his children is to love their mother.

—THEODORE M. HESBURGH, cleric

The joys of parents are secret, and so are their griefs and fears.

—FRANCIS BACON, philosopher

Wisdom for
New Parents

Parenting, at its best, comes as naturally as laughter. It is automatic, involuntary, unconditional love.

—SALLY JAMES, writer

Remember that basic care for babies includes responding to their curiosity drive and their need for stimulation and learning opportunities, just as much as their need to be fed, diapered, bathed, and protected from physical harm. Parents cannot be too caring or too vigilant about the quality of their child's everyday experiences.

—CRAIG T. RAMEY AND SHARON L. RAMEY,
child-development experts and writers

When a baby looks into a caregiver's face—that person's, that mother's, that father's—it's the map of that child's world. And if those maps are always changing, that world can become very frightening.

—FRED ROGERS, TV personality

The walks and talks we have with our two-year-olds in red boots have a great deal to do with the values they will cherish as adults.

—EDITH F. HUNTER, writer

Exploring nature with your child is largely a matter of becoming receptive to what lies around you.

—RACHEL CARSON, biologist, ecologist, and writer

All too often as parents we take the role of directing everything from breakfast to bath time to bedtime. When it comes to play, follow your child's lead. Let him be in control and determine the play. Relax—it's fun not to be in charge.

—ANNE K. BLOCKER, registered dietitian and writer

Here's how to change from being a workman to being a child: Take off your business suit, sit on the floor, ignore the phone, and make a fool of yourself.

—Zoe Stern, writer

Especially if you're not able to make a great deal of time for your baby, it's important to make the most of the time you do have. Don't read the paper at the breakfast table, sit glued to the six o'clock news before dinner, or sleep until noon on Saturday. Instead, wield the baby spoon at breakfast, give the bath at six o'clock, take the baby to the playground on Saturday morning.

—Arlene Eisenberg, Heidi E. Murkoff,
and Sandee E. Hathaway,
What To Expect The First Year

71

The darn trouble with cleaning the house is it gets dirty the next day anyway, so skip a week if you have to. The children are the most important thing.

—BARBARA BUSH, first lady

[The point is that] children need to feel a relaxed sense of availability. They have to be able to take parents for granted. When they do, they have the security that when they come and go, there is a base to come back to.

—T. BERRY BRAZELTON AND STANLEY I. GREENSPAN, pediatricians and writers

If the motto of real estate is "Location, location, location," the motto of parenting is "Consistency, consistency, consistency."... The idea is to have very few rules but to enforce them every single time.

—DR. DENIS DONOVAN, physician and writer

Wise mothers and fathers rebuke and praise just to the right degree.

—Dr. Frank Crane, writer

Don't tolerate temper tantrums. Not now. Not when he's 15. The world won't.

—Harry H. Harrison, Jr., writer

Few sinners are saved after the first 20 minutes of a sermon.

—Mark Twain, writer and humorist

Loving a child doesn't mean giving in to all his whims; to love him is to bring out the best in him, to teach him to love what is difficult.

—Nadia Boulanger, music teacher

Teach him that there's a direct correlation between studying and good grades.

—HARRY H. HARRISON, JR., writer

Discipline is a symbol of caring to a child.... If you have never been hated by your child, you have never been a parent.

—BETTE DAVIS, actor

It is better to bind your children to you by a feeling of respect, and by gentleness, than by fear.

—TERENCE, Roman playwright

Respect the child. Be not too much his parent. Trespass not on his solitude.

—RALPH WALDO EMERSON, writer and philosopher

The thing you learn about children is that you can't change them.

—MICK JAGGER, rock star

I've learned that you should always take time to answer little children when they ask "why?"

—ANONYMOUS

Level with your child by being honest. Nobody spots a phony quicker than a child.

—MARY MACCRACKEN, writer

Teach him nothing that he ever does—or is going to do—is worth lying to you about.

—HARRY H. HARRISON, JR., writer

Never teach your child to be cunning for you may be certain you will be one of the very first victims of his shrewdness.

—JOSH BILLINGS, humorist

The best brought-up children are those who have seen their parents as they are; hypocrisy is not the parents' first duty.

—GEORGE BERNARD SHAW, dramatist

Don't lie—If you hear yourself saying, "It won't hurt, sweetie!" bite your tongue. Always tell your children as much of the truth as they can understand, if not out of a fundamental moral imperative, then at least in an effort to establish and maintain the most valuable attribute you have as a parent—your credibility.

—STAN AND JAN BERENSTAIN,
writers and creators of the Berenstain Bears

I've learned that you can't expect your child to listen to your advice and ignore your example.

—ANONYMOUS

Children need models rather than critics.

—JOSEPH JOUBERT, ethicist and essayist

Children have never been very good at listening to their elders, but they have never failed to imitate them.

—JAMES BALDWIN, writer

"Walk the walk" matters. Children learn what they live. They learn from what they see and hear their parents *do*—how parents make things work, how they solve problems, what behavior is acceptable or not, what types of cues and words win positive responses. Parents can and do mentor through their everyday actions and words.

—CRAIG T. RAMEY AND SHARON L. RAMEY,
child-development experts and writers

Train a child in the way he should go, and when he is old he will not turn from it.

—PROVERBS

Experience has taught me that nothing is more useful to parents than gentleness and affability.

—TERENCE, Roman playwright

Play together and pray together.

—IRISH SAYING

The best things you can give children, next to good habits, are good memories.

—SYDNEY J. HARRIS, journalist and writer

You have to love your children unselfishly. That's hard. But it's the only way.

—BARBARA BUSH, first lady

Parents must have a tender heart,
    an inflexible will,
And, the patience and faith of saints.

—FRENCH SAYING

Children are likely to live up to what you believe of them.

—LADY BIRD JOHNSON, first lady

The parents exist to teach the child, but also they must learn what the child has to teach them; and the child has a very great deal to teach them.

—ARNOLD BENNETT, novelist and playwright

Don't get so involved in the duties of your life and your children that you forget the pleasure. Remember why you had children.

—LOIS WYSE, writer

Perhaps parents would enjoy their children more if they stopped to realize that the film of childhood can never be run through for a second showing.

—EVELYN NOWN, writer

If you want your children to turn out well, spend twice as much time with them, and half as much money.

—ABIGAIL VAN BUREN, advice columnist

Teach your children to embrace life as an experience filled with endless possibilities for positively affecting the quality of their lives and for transforming the world.

—STEVEN CARR REUBEN,
child-development specialist and writer

Growth, character, and enjoyment of life come from our mistakes. A child that is not permitted to fall will never learn to walk, for walking is a succession of falls.

—DR. FRANK CRANE, writer

A child who constantly hears "Don't," "Be careful," "Stop" will eventually be overtaken by school-mates, business associates, and rival suitors.

—MARCELENE COX, columnist

If there is anything that we wish to change in the child, we should first examine it and see whether it is not something that could better be changed in ourselves.

—CARL JUNG, psychiatrist

All children wear the sign: "I want to be important NOW." Many of our juvenile delinquency problems arise because nobody reads the signs.

—DAN PURSUIT, educator

If you bungle raising your children, I don't think whatever else you do well matters very much.

—JACQUELINE KENNEDY ONASSIS, first lady and editor

Don't let these parenting years get away from you. Your contributions to your children and grandchildren could rank as your greatest accomplishments in life.

—DR. JAMES DOBSON, pediatrician, educator, and writer

The future of the world would be assured if every child was loved.

—DR. BERNIE SIEGEL, pediatric surgeon and writer